Take a Hint

I0449618

Take a Hint

John R. O'Neon

Lulu.com

First edition published 2008 by Lulu.com

The right of John R. O'Neon to be identified as the
Author of this work has been asserted by him in accordance
With the copyright, design and patents Act 1988.

ISBN 978-1-4092-2212-5

Dedicated to the ones I love

Time is the moment that lasted forever
And the day that disappeared

*

As long as we have memories
Yesterday remains
As long as we have hope
Tomorrow waits

Also by
John R. O'Neon

Enigmas
Maria's Revenge
Karn's Chronicle
1900 hours
Bast
Granny & Granddads
Household Encyclopedia

Take a Hint

WHEN your gravy tastes too salty, remove the salty taste by adding a pinch or two of brown sugar.

PREVENT artichokes from turning pots grey by soaking them in a tablespoonful of vinegar before cooking.

FRESHEN limp lettuce by placing it in water with a teaspoonful of vinegar added. Leave for a couple of minutes then shake well.

REJUVENATE discolored surfaces by mixing a cup of water with a tablespoonful of bleach and vinegar, place in the pan and simmer for 5 -1O minutes. Wash and rinse item, then dry thoroughly.

WHEN cutting roses from a bush and you have no gloves hold the branch with a clothes peg and prevent fingers from getting pricked.

WHEN thinly sliced meat is needed, freeze the meat slightly until it is firm, then with a sharp knife cut thin slices easily and quickly.

FREEZE your oranges and lemons before you need to grate them, it makes it easier.

USE an old lampshade frame fixed firmly into a flower pot for trailers like ivy for indoor gardens.

GREEN tomatoes will ripen more quickly if placed in a brown paper bag.

IF your high pile shag carpet has become flattened, raise it by running a garden rake back and forth over it.

ALWAYS keep books on the front of the shelves, never push them to the back. Air circulating around the books will prevent them from getting musty.

IF books become damp, sprinkle some talcum powder over the pages to absorb the moisture. When they are dry, thoroughly clean off the powder.

STAINS of fresh lipstick can often be removed from clothing by wiping gently with a piece of fresh white bread.

STOPPERS getting stuck in decanters can be a problem. Usually all that is needed is a gentle tap with another glass object to remove them, if this doesn't work, try a few drops of glycerin around the stopper and leave for a few minutes then remove.

PREVENT your sponge mop from drying and cracking, wrap it in a plastic bag after use. You will be surprised how much longer it will last.

STOP garlic and ginger from shooting, store them in airtight containers in the fridge.

PREVENT cracker biscuits from breaking by placing them on a thick slice of bread to butter.

ICING for chocolate cake will not moisten on the cake if you add a teaspoonful of corn flour to the icing sugar and cocoa.

WHEN adding flavoring to cakes and biscuits always add with the creamed butter and sugar. This allows the flavor time to develop before cooking.

WHEN frying with deep fat only add a few pieces at a time to the boiling fat/oil. The temperature is reduced and the food will not crisp if its all put in at once.

STAINLESS steel can be cleaned by wiping with a cloth moistened in vinegar, rinse thoroughly and dry well.

LEFTOVER scones make lovely dumplings if they are placed on top of stews or steak and kidney for the last 10 minutes of cooking.

BEFORE having new carpet laid on a timber floor, wash the boards with water and turpentine. Moths hate the smell and will stay away.

GET a better grip on fish when skinning them by dipping your fingers in salt.

AN old remedy for nappy rash that really works is

to use corn flour instead of talcum powder. It soothes the sting in minutes.

WHEN potting plants, cut a small disc of soft foam to fit the inside of the pot. This helps retain the dirt, the water drains away slowly and it retains some moisture for the plants.

EQUAL parts of olive oil, methylated spirits and vinegar mixed together makes a wonderful furniture restorer.

OLD interlock singlet's and nightgowns make very good dusters, just cut with pinking shears.

PROTECT the backs of mirrors by giving them a coat of varnish.

BOOT polish stains on the ankles of stockings can be removed by using methylated spirits.

REMOVE the smell of fish from your hands by rubbing them with some dry mustard, will also remove the fish smell from cutlery if added to the washing up water.

IF you like the taste of cucumber but want to avoid the indigestion that follows, slice the cucumber and sprinkle with salt. Leave to drain then rinse before using.

PREVENT the leaves of your lettuce from going brown by tearing apart with your hands, do not use a knife.

TO clean household china, especially cracked china, soak in household bleach for a few hours, rinse thoroughly.

KEEP stray dogs and cats away from your garden beds, grate a small amount of soap and scatter the pieces about the garden. Dogs and cats dislike the smell of soap.

JARS of cream will go twice as far if you whip it and fold in a stiffly beaten egg just before serving.

RUB some butter over the wire cake rack before turning a cake out, the cake will not stick and will not leave marks.

ADD a deliciously different flavor to rhubarb, add a few passion fruit when cooking.

IF you have a nylon or brass zip that has become too stiff to work freely, close it and run a lead pencil up and down it several times.

WHEN keeping hard boiled eggs in the refrigerator, place the eggs in a jug of water, this will prevent the 'egg' odour that comes from them.

SCRATCHES on enamel stove tops. Put some neat bleach and leave until the area whitens. Remove bleach and wash thoroughly with fresh Detergent and then polish.

SCREW TOP jars that will not open, hold a piece of sandpaper around the lid, if still stuck hold the lid in hot water.

WHEN knitting, be sure not to cast off to tightly by using a larger sized needle.

BEFORE washing tea stained linen, rub a little glycerin into each stain, when washed will be white again.

AN aspirin in a vase makes flowers last longer.

SUITS or coats that have developed a shiny patch can be improved by brushing with a solution of warm water and ammonia.

COLD tea water is good for mirrors, just dampen a cloth and wipe over.

WHEN shopping at whatever time of the year, watch out for items that you could use for Christmas presents, this saves a mad rush at Xmas

CARROTS stay fresh for weeks if wrapped in a paper bag, then wrap again with plastic film.

WHEN ironing, use hot water to dampen the clothes, hot water penetrates the fabric better than cold.

WHEN defrosting the freezer, wrap your meat in clean newspaper it will stay frozen longer.

TO peel small onions and keep them whole for cooking, simply immerse them in boiling water for one minute. The skin will peel off very quickly and easily.

REMOVE the odour of onions from a wooden chopping board by rubbing the board with salt.

TO prevent soggy pastry in fruit tarts, sprinkle the bottom and sides of the pastry case with a mixture of sugar and flour before you put the fruit in.

KEEP tomato paste that has been left over, place in a small container and pour a layer of oil over the top. Place in the fridge and it will stay fresh for days.

EPSOM SALTS has a variety of uses: it helps the growth of lettuce if sprinkled around when planting. It will also help keep woolens free from moths. And if dissolved in warm water, it will help whiten some yellowed clothes.

PREVENT lightweight vases from toppling over, place some pebbles in the bottom of the vase, this will also allow short-stemmed flowers to appear taller.

RUB the stoppers of hot water bottles with Vaseline and they will turn more easily.

ADD a few drops of glycerin to new hot-water bottles when filling with water. This will help keep them more flexible and they will last much longer.

ADD a mashed banana when making fish cakes for a delicious flavor.

USE fruit juice in a meat casserole instead of water to give it a delightful flavor for children.

ALWAYS turn woolens inside out before placing in the dryer to prevent them from becoming fluffy.

LINE shoe cupboards with blotting paper to prevent mildew forming.

WHEN baking custard add a few marshmallows. they rise to the top and make a delicious meringue.

GET rid of onion-weed in your garden by sprinkling with turpentine.

A teaspoonful of salt added to the water will stop a cracked egg from boiling out into the water.

KEEP the cat off of your favorite chair, stuff a couple of moth balls down the side, cats hate the smell.

WHEN making garlic butter give it an extra zing by adding grated parmesan cheese.

HELP keep woolens in their original shape, always rinse with water at the same temperature that you washed with. If the shape is important lay flat on a sheet of paper and draw a line around the outline, then place the garment on the outline to dry.

USE an old fashioned toast rack as a letter rack, handy and attractive.

ADD starch to rinsing water when washing tea

towels, they will not leave fluff and lint on glassware.

TO clean suede handbags, shoes and even jackets, make a solution of warm water with white laundry powder added. Lightly sponge the article with a wrung out sponge or towel.

SQUEEZE a drop of lemon juice into rice while cooking, this will help whiten and separate the grains.

APPLY clear nail varnish to the ends of children's hair ribbons to stop them from fraying.

ADD a little salt when cooking Prunes for improved flavor.

A dusting of corn flour in shoes will keep them fresh and ease your feet.

RUB the soles of baby shoes with a cut raw potato and he/she won't slip on polished floors.

ALWAYS polish new shoes before wearing, this increases the suppleness and protects them against spotting in the rain.

NEVER clean damp shoes as this sets the stain, allow to dry first.

MIX mustard with mayonnaise for a delightful change of taste.

RUB a raw onion on chilblains to give quick relief.

WHEN using fondant on fruit cakes, roll out on heavy duty plastic and it will not tear or crack when transferred to the cake.

ALUMINIUM saucepans can be cleaned of stains by boiling passion fruit skins in them.

A few drops of lemon juice on your tooth brush will whiten your teeth.

ADD one or two oxtail soup cubes to plain minced beef and onion. It is delicious and also thickens.

ADD half a cup of coconut to the jam for a tart, makes the jam go a lot further and the tart easier to cut.

RUB tea stains on china with vinegar and salt to remove.

CLEAN straw matting with a solution of salt and water. It also prevents it turning yellow.

KEEP a plastic bag close to the phone when making cakes and slip it over your hand when it rings to pick up the receiver.

PREVENT musty smells in silver teapots that are unused by placing a couple of sugar lumps inside. Sugar also keeps vacuum flasks smelling sweet.

KEEP small objects like fondue and cake forks from falling through the basket in a dishwasher, place a pot scrubber in the bottom and stick the objects into it.

SHOES will stay whiter longer if the whitening polish is mixed with a small amount of milk instead of water.

MAKE excellent bath mats, Place a sheet of foam rubber between two toweling tea towels and stitch around the edges. They make great gifts for stalls and fetes.

WHEN making knitted tea cozies, line the inside with aluminum foil. The foil keeps the tea hotter a lot longer.

SOFTEN dried fruit especially prunes, soak them

overnight in a flask full of hot water.

SOAK your gold chains in methylated spirits. They simply sparkle.

LIGHT scuff marks can be removed from light-colored leather shoes with an art Gum Eraser. Available from most stationery stores.

HANG a match-stick blind on the wall of the family room or kitchen; it can be used to display children's works of art without harming walls.

NYLON netting is a very useful cleaning aid in the bathroom or kitchen. It also removes bugs from car windscreens; it's a gentle abrasive and will not scratch.

FOR a moist non-crumbly coconut cake, soak the coconut in milk for 30 minutes before using.

FOR a more nutritious and flavorsome white sauce, use powdered milk and the water from cooked vegetables.

CAULIFLOWER will stay white and there will be fewer odour's if you place a piece of white bread in the saucepan during cooking.

KEEP you're jogging shoes pleasant smelling, apply a drop of eucalyptus oil from an eye dropper about once a week.

TREAT areas where there is wood worm and borer with kerosene sprayed into the holes.
ADD 1 tablespoonful of corn flour to scone mixture, your scones will be lighter and keep fresher longer.

BEFORE wearing new shoes rub the inside heels with a piece of soap. It will stop feet from blistering.

LEATHER chairs can be kept in good condition by rubbing over with linseed oil from time to time, it cleanses and nourishes the leather.

IT is a good idea after oiling your sewing machine, to machine through at least two layers of blotting paper until no more oil appears, this will save your work being ruined.

FOR colour and piquancy with cauliflower. Add 2 tablespoons of chopped mustard pickle to 1 pint of cream sauce when serving.

ADD a little borax to the water when next washing your hair it not only softens the water but adds shine to your hair.

SEW carrot seeds thickly in a low bowel for an attractive table decoration. They grow quickly and can be trimmed to any shape.

POWDERED milk sprinkled onto scones before putting them in the oven gives them a golden crust and saves glazing.

QUICK chocolate sauce. Mix 1 tablespoon condensed milk, 1 dessertspoon cocoa and I dessertspoon of fresh milk and beat well.

USES for vinegar. Brown vinegar with a small amount of salt will clean the dirtiest copper like new. Place Bi-carb' soda in the sink or drain and pour down ½ cup of vinegar, let it gurgle and bubble then pour down boiling water for sweet smelling drains. Also ideal for... insect bites, and takes the burn out of sunburn like magic.

TRY leaving out a teaspoon of flour from a sponge cake recipe and substituting an amount of Arrowroot, this greatly improves texture.

PREVENT sinking of a sponge cake; add 2 teaspoons of cold water to eggs and sugar mixture, beating will also be easier. Cut sponge cakes with a cotton thread instead of a knife.

MAKE a ball of plain flour mixed with cleaning fluid. Use to clean the stubborn marks off of wallpaper, rub gently.

SOAK sweet stained garments in salt water or White vinegar before washing.

GIVE each member of your family a small nylon bag to place there soiled socks in, place them all in the washing machine and they come out clean and presorted.

KEEP waxed paper handy to your ironing board, run your iron over it and then dash it over a clean towel, makes the iron glide lovely over your clothes.

WHITE socks that never seem to come white

again will if soaked in boiling water with a slice of lemon before washing.

WHEN you store your woolens away in the summer, use newspaper as moths don't like printers ink.

AN apple corer makes a quick and neat job of removing the small circle in the tops of patty cakes you intend to fill with jam or cream.

TO remove grass stains from clothes, dampen the article and sprinkle it with sugar. Leave it overnight and then wash in the usual way.

REMOVE wrinkles from ties by inserting a piece of cardboard inside the tie, place cheesecloth over and press with a steam iron.

DOUBLE sets of photographs often go to waste. Use them as postcards to friends you haven't seen for a while.

STORE mushrooms in empty egg cartons in the fridge to keep them fresh and dry much longer.

A quick and easy desert when entertaining: make a chocolate box from after-dinner mints, melt the edges together inside a cake tin, freeze and fill with cream or ice cream and whatever else you wish.

PLACE an open container of bicarbonate of soda inside your refrigerator to help absorb odours and keep the fridge sweet smelling. Replace the bicarb' every six weeks.

WELL loved pieces of china can become cracked and look ugly and dirty. You can eliminate the dirt by dabbing the cracks with a cotton bud dipped in peroxide. Make sure that you rinse thoroughly after applying it.

TO make all glassware and crystal sparkle, wash in water with a little vinegar added.

BEFORE storing silver after cleaning, wrap in it in aluminum foil and it will not tarnish.

TEA leaves and vinegar shaken in a cloudy decanter will help remove the sediment film.

BORAX is good for removing obstinate stains from porcelain baths. Mix to a paste with a little ammonia.

DISSOLVE a little camphor in the water when cleaning mirrors. Flies will not rest on them after this treatment.

TO quickly remove the smell of burnt food from the kitchen, sprinkle a little cinnamon in a saucepan and heat it. Remove from the heat and allow it to cool.

SPILLED food in the oven? Simply sprinkle with salt immediately, when the oven has cooled wipe it out with warm water.

AVOID crease marks in shirt collars by ironing from each peak towards the centre of the back of collar.

KEEP a few clothes pegs in your kitchen drawer, they are very handy to keep packets of cereals, biscuits and flour closed.

IF you drop a raw egg on the floor, sprinkle it with salt and leave for a few minutes. You will then be able to sweep it up with a broom.

CLEAN grease and dirt marks from wallpaper by wiping over with a piece of white bread.

WHEN reheating cooked food, place a pan of water on the bottom of the oven, this prevents the food from drying out.

PREVENT a cake from drying out to quickly, place half an apple in the cake tin. The cake will keep deliciously moist a lot longer.

SPRINKLE sawdust around seedlings when planting out to save them from snails.

WHEN whipping cream for cakes add a pinch of bi- carb' soda. It will stay fresh for days.

WHEN crumbing fish or cutlets, brush the fish with oil and the crumbs will stick firmly.

TO stop rissoles from cracking and breaking during cooking, always shape each one with wet hands, or dip each one in water before rolling in flour.

CLEAN aluminum saucepans by cooking a few sticks
of rhubarb in them.

USE a wad of steel wool instead of paper to block up a mouse hole. Mice can't chew through the steel.

AFTER washing a rarely used table cloth, fold it the wrong way round for storing. If the creases become soiled they will not show when used.

WHEN removing buttons from garments slip a fork between the button and the fabric and you will not damage the garment.

WHEN cleaning strapped sandals place your hand into a plastic bag first, you won't polish your hands.

WHEN making batter for fish, try adding ¼ teaspoon of dry mustard for a pleasant and tasty change.

LEMON juice is a good substitute for vinegar in mint sauce and salad dressings.

CLEAN stubborn stains off fish tanks and ovens by running a disposable razor up and down the glass.

WHEN boiling a pudding in a cloth, place half a lemon into the water. It will come away from the cloth without sticking.

UNSIGHTLY hem marks that show after a dress has been lengthened can be dealt with by rubbing the inside of the material with a cloth moistened in salt, then ironed. The marks will simply disappear.

WHEN painting steps or stairs that are in constant use, paint alternate steps and allow to dry before painting the others. The steps can always be used.

TENDERIZE steak by rubbing it with lemon juice or French dressing about one hour before cooking.

FOR a delicious flavor to cooked spinach, add a small amount of peanut butter and mix through.

LAMBS fry, to prevent it from becoming tough, dip each piece into some milk, completely cover it, lift out and place into fat without draining it stops it from becoming leathery.

PUT a piece of dripping about the size of a walnut in the water in which greens are cooking, it prevents them from boiling over.

SOAK dentures in a cup of water and add ¼ cup white vinegar. Use once a week and brush in the usual way.

ROLL rissoles in whole meal flour before frying, it gives a crisp nutty flavor.

WHEN cooking corned beef always place in cold water with a slice of lemon. 1 tablespoon vinegar. 1 teaspoon dry mustard.

REVIVE Holland blinds with a coat of flat plastic paint to match the surrounding wall, apply evenly to both sides.

KEEP putty in a workable condition indefinitely by wrapping it in some aluminum foil.

IMPROVE the flavor of cabbage by adding a little grated apple at cooking time.

WHEN moving heavy furniture around slip old socks over the legs of the item, this will prevent any scratches on your floor.

WHEN you make Rum Ba-Ba cake, after cooking prick all over with a metal skewer. Then pour the rum over and allow it to soak into the holes. it will be delicious.

WHEN packing or storing pleated skirts, pull them through discarded nylon stockings with the feet cut away. This ensures the pleats will be kept in position.

WHEN traveling, slip your shoes into old socks, it saves soiling your clothes.

TOP-and-tail bananas and bake them in their skins, they are excellent when served with grills or chicken dishes.

TO clean aluminum cutlery, soak in boiling water with 2 teaspoons of cream of tarter added. Rinse well and wipe.

GIVE homemade marmalade a delicious flavor by adding l25g chopped and preserved ginger before... cooking. Ginger mixed with chopped dates also makes tasty sandwich fillings.

CARDBOARD rolls from kitchen foil popped into the arms of newly washed sweaters will help speed up the drying process.

KEEP bananas fresh for up to 3 weeks by wrapping them up in as much as six layers of newspaper and keep them in the fridge.

DON'T discard your old Christmas cards, cut out the picture and use them as gift tags on parcels, tie or stick on with tape or cotton.

PREVENT the bathroom mirror from steaming up when showering or having a bath by wiping over the mirror with a cloth moistened in equal amounts of glycerin and methylated spirits.

TRY scenting sheets and pillowcases by putting a tablespoon of bath salts in the rinsing water.

PEEL oranges and any citrus fruits quickly and easily by putting them into very hot water for five minutes.

WHEN cooking corn add a dash of sugar not salt, salt will toughen the kernels.

WHEN a tissue accidentally gets into the washing machine and makes a mess over dark clothing, simply place the clothes in the dryer for ten minutes (no heat required) they will come out lint free.

CLEAN your blender, place some detergent with some hot water into it and blend for about one minute, rinse thoroughly. It will sparkle.

WHEN thickening soups and casseroles add a cupful of rolled oats to each liter of liquid, for the last hour of... ...cooking. This makes a well balanced meal and thickens beautifully.

QUICK and easy to make chutney, add some vinegar (to taste) to apricot jam, then add a pinch of cayenne pepper and mix well.

CROCHET around the edges of souvenir tea-towels and place them across the backs of chairs, they protect and visitors will love to discuss them.

ADD flavor and crispness to fried fish by adding half vinegar and water to the self raising flour used in the batter.

KEEP an old ice cream bucket or similar in your car and place your wet umbrella in it and the carpet will stay dry.

KEEP biscuits from becoming moist by putting a piece of bread in the container with them.

SAVE time when making biscuits, roll mixture into shape of a sausage and cut in slices, shape and mark with fork.

SOAK a cold joint of meat in salted water for an hour before re-heating, it will taste freshly cooked.

POACHED eggs will keep for several days if they are covered with water and kept in the fridge, when required they can be placed in boiling water for about one minute. Serve straight away.

TO clean the leaves on your African Violets, use a soft blusher brush. It is ideal for these delicate beauties.

YOU will extend the life of nylon hosiery by washing it in cold water.

TAKE away the pain of a Bee sting by dabbing honey on the area after removing the sting.

GREASE and flour cake tins and place them in the fridge for a few hours before using; cakes will never stick to the bottom.

BEFORE placing socks in the washing machine, secure them together with a safety pin, this eliminates searching for that elusive odd sock.

GARLIC, onions and parsley planted around rose bushes will help deter aphids.

NEXT time you go on a picnic take a shower curtain with you instead of a rug! It doesn't matter if it gets wet, spills wipe up easily, you can wrap the leftovers in it and it washes out easy afterwards.

FOR quick and easy seafood sauce, mix equal amounts of tomato sauce and mayonnaise together.

IF your curry dish is to hot simply add some natural yoghurt, stir in gently.

TO dust Venetian blinds slip an old pair of socks over your hands and slide between the slats.

GROW mint in large pots near both back and front doors to help keep flies away.

TRY folding beaten egg whites into milk pudding. It makes light and ideal nourishment for invalids.

WHEN picking tomatoes leave 25mm of stem on the fruit and it will retain its flavor.

BEFORE cooking rolled oats melt a small piece of butter with a pinch of salt in the saucepan to keep the oats from sticking to the bottom.

TEA towels can be kept an excellent colour by putting the rind of a lemon in the water you wash them in.

HANG a bag of camphor inside the piano. it absorbs dampness and prevents moths from attacking the felt hammers and dampers.

HAVING trouble with mildew? Line your drawers, cupboards, wardrobes and shoe boxes with blotting paper.

PLACE a dab of blue tack under the bottom frame of
a picture to keep it hanging straight.

REMOVE nicotine stains from your fingers by applying nail varnish remover. It will remove other stubborn stains as well.

IF and when you go into hospital, take a pretty blouse in place of a bed jacket, you will feel a lot better and get a lot more wear from it.

AFTER painting pour a little of the paint into an old nail polish bottle, the brush is just the right size to cover those scratches and chips when needed.

ADD variety and tang to scones by adding a tablespoon of fruit yoghurt to the scone dough. When mixing use less milk, the scones will be light and fluffy in texture.

A quick Chinese style soup, make up a packet of chicken noodle soup according to direction, then five minutes before serving, break an egg into it together with some chopped lettuce.

TO clean bricks around the fireplace, scrub with white vinegar, sponge off with warm water.

IF you apply perfume when your body is still moist after showering, the effect will be better and last longer.

YOU should store your perfumes in a cool dark place, they will last longer. They deteriorate

quickly in warm bathrooms and on dressing tables.

DO not add salt to greens until almost cooked. this will ensure a fresh colour without using soda.

WHEN making chocolate cakes always add a teaspoon of coffee essence to bring out the flavour.

IF plain cake has gone stale, cut into fingers, butter, sprinkle with some coconut and toast.

ADD a tablespoon of melted chocolate to the treacle when making gingerbread for a delicious flavor.

FOR the gourmet touch add a wineglass of sherry to clear soup just before serving.

AFTER peeling and slicing onions leave in milk for l5 minutes and they will fry to a delicious brown.

TO avoid odours when cooking cabbage, cauliflower and Brussels sprouts, simply add a teaspoon of sugar to the water.

POUR the syrup from tinned fruits into ice-cube trays and freeze. They are delicious when added to your unsweetened soft drinks. They can also be made into lollipops for children, simply put a stick in and freeze.

ON button through skirts and dresses, sew the bottom button on with elastic. This will prevent stress on the material and stop a tear.

WHEN knitting jackets or cardigans for newborn babies, make the button holes in both front bands, the garment will then be ready when the baby is born and the buttons can be added to the appropriate side.

BEFORE buying fish, check it has a clean scent. It should not have a strong fishy flavour if fresh.

The flesh should be firm to the touch and the eyes shiny and bright.

IF you do not intend to cook fresh fish immediately, keep it in the fridge on a bed of ice and cover loosely with some waxed paper. This will keep it fresh another day or two.

SERVE fresh parsley fried crisply with fried fish, it's delicious.

CURRY powder sprinkled onto the pan when frying fish helps prevent a strong odour and improves the flavor of the fish.

WRAP cheese between two cabbage leaves and it will keep fresh in the fridge for months.

TO hang a long evening dress without it scraping the floor, sew two loops into the waist, turn inside out and hang up like a skirt.

TO prevent clothes from slipping off wooden and plastic hangers, stick a piece of foam rubber at each end of the hanger.

USE carpet samples or small leftover pieces to protect your table tops when using typewriters or sewing machines. They will also help muffle the sound from computers as well.

PREVENT white table linen from becoming yellow; wrap it in blue tissue paper when stored.

DIP a paddle pop stick into left over paint, tape it to the side of the tin, you can use it as a colour code match when going out shopping for more.

OLD ceramic tiles make very decorative and protective mats for your table and kitchen counter, use a self adhesive pad in each corner.

PLASTIC containers that tooth brushes come in are excellent for storing crochet hooks and needles.

KEEP carved wood free of dust by using an old soft toothbrush to clean instead of a cloth.

AFTER washing and drying cast iron pans, place them in a warm oven to dry thoroughly. Moisture makes cast iron deteriorate more quickly.

TO make steam puddings that are light as a feather, replace half of the flour called for with bread crumbs.

WHEN boiling sago for children add golden syrup instead of sugar. It gives a delicious flavour.

WHEN making coleslaw add a little chopped, tinned or fresh pineapple. it adds greatly to the flavor.

ARTHRITIS: Eat a l5cm. Stick of celery each day.

TO add a delicious flavor to mashed potatoes, mix with mayonnaise instead of milk and butter.

KEEP your mending basket close to the phone, then if you get into a lengthy conversation you can also get some mending done.

SWEET potatoes tend to discolor when boiled but this can be prevented by adding a little milk to the boiling water. And when baking them, dip them in milk and dust lightly with flour. Do not use salt, it adds to the discoloring.

ADD a few drops of lavender oil (or concentrate of your choice) in the vacuum cleaner bag leaves a lovely fragrance around the house as you clean.

SAVE cutting into your hands with plastic shopping bags, take a four-inch length of garden

hose slit down its length and put the bag handles inside it for blister free shopping.

ELIMINATE odours from the kitchen waste-disposal unit; feed some fresh mint through it.

MAKE sticky tape extra strong; place it in the fridge before use

FREEZE cooking tomatoes until solid then rinse in hot water for easy peeling.

DON'T throw out old nail varnish brushes; after cleaning in polish remover, they can be used for painting fiddly objects, gluing and even cleaning small things.

STORE meat and fish scraps in plastic bags in your freezer until garbage day. Your garbage will now stay fresher with no flies or pets rummaging.

CUTOUTS from old birthday cards make pretty bedroom mobiles.

OLD stockings are very useful craft items; with thin wire, rubber bands and glue they can form butterflies.

TO avoid burning your hands when cutting chilies, rub oil into the hands before starting the job.

IF you have a bottle of milk that's almost near its expiry date, don't throw it away! Add a teaspoon of vanilla essence to it and it will keep for several more days.

TO sharpen dull scissors, cut a piece of aluminum foil several times.

TO use up leftover croissants, sweet or savoury, use them in a bread and butter pudding, adding the usual dried fruits and flavourings.

SKID PROOF a new concrete path, scratch over with a stiff bristled brush just before the concrete sets.

ADD ammonia to turpentine and use to remove paint from clothing, it's more effective.

TO air sheets for unexpected guests, place them in the dryer for about ten minutes with a scented handkerchief.

WHEN planting flower bulbs that need lifting after flowering, plant them in wire mesh. When the plant has died it's easy to locate and pull from the ground.

WHEN pinning a garment for a fitting use small safety pins instead of straight pins, they don't fall out and don't stick in the person.

RUB dampened mint onto your legs and arms in the summer months to help deter flies. They hate it.

DON'T discard leftover black coffee, pour into ice cube trays and freeze, the next time you serve iced coffee, the... coffee cubes retain the real flavour without weakening the drink.

A piece of charcoal placed in muslin bags and popped inside of cupboards will absorb any dampness.

A block of camphor stored in unused luggage will keep it smelling sweet and prevent dampness.

TO protect your gas or electricity stove from 'spatters ' run a length of foil over the surface and

cut holes for the burners, satisfactory and cheaper than aluminum trays.

WHEN pegging pantyhose on the line, drop a marble inside the foot, this will stop them getting tangled and laddered.

IF your plants are looking jaded, place a few tiny pieces of washing soda into the soil. Do not let it touch the roots. they will soon perk up.

CANDLES that have gotten bent can be straightened by placing inside a plastic bag and holding under hot water, then roll on a flat surface.

AFTER peeling and slicing onions leave in milk for 15 minutes and they will fry to a delicious brown.

DISSOLVE one teaspoon of gelatine in hot water and add to the icing for lamingtons. Icing sets quickly and will not penetrate the cake.

ADD a slice of fruit cake when making curry instead of the usual raisins and sultanas.

REMOVE the odours in your oven after cleaning by turning the oven to a medium heat and placing some orange peel inside, turn the oven off after a few minutes and leave the peel to cool before removing.

POACHED eggs will keep for several days if they are covered with water and kept in the fridge, when... needed they can be placed in boiling water for about one minute, serve straight away.

TO clean the leaves on your African Violets, use a soft blusher brush. It is ideal for these delicate beauties.

YOU will extend the life of nylon hosiery by washing it in cold water.

TAKE away the pain of a bee sting by dabbing honey on the area after removing the sting.

GREASE and flour cake tins and place them in the fridge for a few hours before using, cakes will never stick to the bottom.

BEFORE placing socks in the washing machine, secure them together with a safety pin, this eliminates searching for that elusive odd sock.

GARLIC, onions and parsley planted around rose bushes will help deter aphids.

NEXT time you go on a picnic take a shower curtain with you instead of a rug! It doesn't matter if it gets wet, spills wipe up easily, you can wrap the leftovers in it and it washes out easy afterwards.

FOR quick and easy seafood sauce, mix equal amounts of tomato sauce and mayonnaise together.

IF your curry dish is to hot simply add some natural yoghurt, stir in gently.

TO dust Venetian blinds slip an old pair of socks over your hands and slide between the slats.

GROW mint in large pots near both back and front doors to help keep flies away.

IMPROVE the flavor of cabbage by adding a little grated apple at cooking time.

WHEN moving heavy furniture around slip old socks over the legs of the item, this will prevent any scratches on your floor.

WHEN reheating cooked food, place a pan of water on the bottom of the oven, this prevents the food from drying out.

PREVENT a cake from drying out to quickly, place half an apple in the cake tin. The cake will keep deliciously moist a lot longer.

SPRINKLE sawdust around seedlings when planting out to save them from snails.

WHEN whipping cream for cakes add a pinch of bi-carb soda. It will stay fresh for days.

WHEN crumbing fish or cutlets, add 1 dessertspoon of oil and the crumbs will stick firmly.

TO stop rissoles from cracking and breaking during cooking, always shape each one with wet hands, or dip each one in water before rolling in flour.

CLEAN aluminum saucepans, cook a few sticks of rhubarb in it.

USE a wad of steel wool instead of paper to block up a mouse hole. Mice can't chew through the steel

AFTER washing a rarely used table cloth, fold it the wrong way round for storing. if the creases become soiled they will not show when used.

WHEN removing buttons from garments slip a fork between button and the fabric and you will not damage the garment.

WHEN cleaning strapped sandal's place your hand into a plastic bag first, you won't polish your hands.

WHEN making batter for fish, try adding ¼ teaspoon of dry mustard for a pleasant and tasty change.

LEMON juice is a good substitute for vinegar in mint sauce and salad dressings.

CLEAN stubborn stains off fish tanks and ovens by running a disposable razor up and down the glass.

MAKE a ball of plain flour mixed with cleaning fluid. Use to clean the stubborn marks off of wallpaper, rub gently.

SOAK sweet stained garments in salt water or vinegar (white) water before washing.

GIVE each member of your family a small nylon bag to place there soiled socks in, place them all in the washing machine and they come out clean and presorted.

KEEP waxed paper handy to your ironing board, run your iron over it and then dash it over a clean towel, makes the iron glide lovely over your clothes.

WHITE socks that never seem to come white again will if soaked in boiling water with a slice of lemon before washing.

WHEN you store your woolens away in the summer, use newspaper as moths don't like printers ink.

AN apple corer makes a quick and neat job of removing the small circle in the tops of patty cakes you intend to fill with jam or cream.

TO remove grass stains from clothes, dampen the article and sprinkle it with sugar. Leave it overnight and then wash in the usual way.

REMOVE wrinkles from ties by inserting a piece of cardboard inside the tie, place cheesecloth over and press with a steam iron.

DOUBLE sets of photographs often go to waste. Use them as postcards to friends you haven't seen for a while.

STORE mushrooms in empty egg cartons in the fridge to keep them fresh and dry much longer.

A quick and easy desert when entertaining: make a chocolate box from after-dinner mints, melt the edges together inside a cake tin, freeze and fill with cream or ice cream and whatever else you wish.

VISITING friends with your toddler? Take along some colored pipe cleaners to use as temporary locks to 'off limit' cupboards.

USE leftover fabric from dressmaking to cover wooden coat hangers.

MAKE a simple white board for memos from contact paper over hardboard felt pen marks simple wipe off.

COAT skewers with oil or cooking spray before making kebabs for the barbecue; makes them easy to remove from meat and to clean.

UNCOOKED instant potato is excellent for thickening soups, stews and gravies. Add a little at a time as you stir until you reach the right consistency, no lumps and a great flavour.

AN inexpensive way to clean false teeth is to place them in a cup overnight with half a teaspoon of citric acid in the water.

DON'T put up with salt shakers that don't shake in humid weather, place them in the fridge for a while.

ADD grated carrot to your mashed potatoes for a delicious new flavor as well as having plenty of vitamins.

AVOID making a mess when painting the ceiling, simply cut a hole in a paper plate and slip it over the brush handle, it catches all splatters.

WHEN your boot polish becomes hard don't discard it, add a few drops of mineral turpentine and stir to bring it back to its former consistency.

WHEN painting fences, sprinkle a generous amount of sand on the ground around you, the sand catches the paint drips and can be swept away.

PREVENT pancakes and pikelet's from sticking to the pan, rub the pan over with a raw potato before cooking.

IF you want to remove unwanted print from calico bags, simply sprinkle the printed area with kerosene and leave overnight. Then wash in the usual way.

WHEN potting plants, place a bone in the bottom of the pot to help give extra 'feed' in the latter months. A few pebbles placed around the top also help keep the moisture in and the weeds out.

FOR a tasty thirst quencher on warm days, strain leftover tea into a container with crushed ice, add a teaspoon of sweetener and half of a cup of orange juice. Its nice and low on kilojoules as well.

GIVE mashed potatoes a delicious flavor by adding plain yoghurt instead of butter and milk.

SAND fly bites can be relieved if you rub with brown sugar and a dash of bicarbonate of soda.

OVEN cleaning will be easy if you place a shallow dish of ammonia and water in the oven immediately after roasting. Leave overnight then wash out with hot water with vinegar added.

IF you add a drop of water to the bowl before beating eggs, they will be a lot easier to beat.

IF you can't be bothered to chop nuts for cooking and decorating cakes, simply grind then, in the coffee grinder.

ADD half a cup of nuts to your biscuit mixture, they will be delicious.

IF you have trouble with annoying hiccups, try swallowing a teaspoon of honey, very slowly. Your hiccups will disappear.

WHEN cooking rhubarb, add raspberry jelly instead of sugar, it's delicious and improves the colour.

TO clean gilt picture frames, rub with a cloth moistened in turpentine. When surface dirt is removed use a clean cloth and more oil, finish with a polishing cloth.

WHEN drawer liners have lost their scent, don't discard them, they can be used to wrap gifts.

SCALLOPED edged kitchen tongs are excellent for weeding and cultivating the soil around young plants.

AN inexpensive dessert for hot days can be made by scooping the seeds out of a rock melon. Set a jelly in the centre and place in the fridge. cut into slices and serve when ready.

WHEN coffee goes hard in the jar, don't throw it away, add hot water and shake well, it can be used to flavor cakes and icings as well as making iced coffee drinks.

WHITE shoe polish is excellent for disguising scratches on white walls and ceilings.

NEED Aspic in a hurry? Dissolve 3 teaspoons of gelatin with a meat or vegetable cube stock in half cup of hot water and stir well, Use as desired.

VANILLA beans are excellent for flavoring more than custard, if you snip off about 5 cm and keep it in the biscuits jar, it adds flavor, and a whole bean in the sugar canister adds wonderful aroma.

A Little toothpaste on a clean cloth will remove stains from white shoes, belts, and bags.

WHEN planting very tiny seeds, place them in an old salt shaker. This allows them to drop more evenly.

NEXT time you burn the bottom of a pan, simply place it on to a very cold surface and leave for a few minutes, the burnt on residue will lift out easily.

WHEN making a baked meal, peel potatoes and place in a plastic bag with some bisto, shake well and coat the potatoes and then bake, you will have lovely brown, flavoured potatoes.

WHEN sewing heavy drill or canvas material, rub a little soap over the fabric. This will make the needle sew perfectly without slipping.

WIPE your spectacles with a drop of vinegar on each lens; they will then sparkle without streaking.

AVOID snagging delicate ruffled or pleated lampshades; use an old baby's hair brush. The bristles are soft but effective.

FOR a fast shine on your floor between waxing, put a piece of waxed paper under the mop and slide it over the floor.

ORDINARY fly spray will clean mirrors and windows and also keep flies away.

STAPLE one end of the cardboard rolls that come with foil and plastic, they are excellent for storing sharp knives in.

INSTEAD of washing strawberries in water before use, try in a little white wine. This keeps them crisp and firm.

CLEANING crystal chandeliers? Dip the pendant crystals in Gin for a brilliant result. (Do not drink the gin afterwards.)

TOOTHPASTE and a brush is very good to clean all types of jewelry.

AN easy way to prepare lettuce next time your making a salad, instead of taking it apart leaf by leaf, hold it by the top and tap the bottom smartly on a hard surface, a kitchen bench. Be sure to bring it down straight, you will be able to lift the core out easily.

REMOVE stains on marble topped tables or such with a diluted hydrogen peroxide. Or a paste of bicarbonate of soda and water will also work. You should never use polish on marble it turns it yellow.

RESTORE suede shoes or handbags with a dry carpet shampoo; allow drying then using a suede shoe cleaner.

TO remove grease and oil from mechanics overalls, add sugar to the washing water, it works every time and the result is spotless.

WHEN painting wrought iron railings and gates, use a piece of sponge instead of a brush, it does a better job and is easier to use.

WHEN using a new paint brush run a comb through it several times to remove any loose bristles.

CHEWING gum can be removed from children's hair by rubbing in some peanut butter. When it has loosened, comb it out before shampooing.

IF you use marshmallows to hold candles on cakes you will not get wax on the cake.

OVER ripe bananas can be frozen whole and given to children as lollies

ALMOND oil and olive oil are great hair conditioners. Warm enough oil to cover the scalp and hair and leave in as long as possible before washing out.

PLUCK your eyebrows after a warm shower, the hairs will come out more easily.

FILL a plastic spray bottle with water and use to spray your irritable children in hot weather, it cools them down and is fun as well.

DON'T discard your lemon skins, throw them into your next bath water and relax. You will enjoy the refreshing smell and it helps give you a smooth skin.

WHEN you lift meringues out of the oven, place the tray on to a damp cloth. This will help prevent the meringues from breaking.

IF you prepare salad hours before serving, place a saucer inverted in the bottom of the bowl. the moisture drops and will collect under the saucer and prevent the salad becoming sodden.

WHEN knitting around the necks of jumpers with four needles, slip a cork over the end of the needles to prevent the stitches slipping off.

WHEN dissolving gelatin, add the gelatin to the liquid and not the other way around.

MAKE an inexpensive icing bag with aluminum foil, twist the foil into a cone, snip off the end after filling.

EMPTY butter containers can be used to store unused fruit, meats and other foods.

WHEN reheating a meat pie in the oven, cover the pie with foil and place a dish of water on the shelf below, this keeps the pie moist and will prevent the pastry from hardening.

GLUE a small cork on the inside of your sewing machine drawer, you can keep your thimble on it, saves needle pricks rummaging through it.

TO blanch shelled almonds and peanuts quickly, pour boiling water over them and let stand for a few minutes ...until the skin's are loosened, then slip the skins off with your finger tips.

MEASURE food coloring and flavoring into recipes with a medicine dropper.

TO make a tasty crumb mixture for sausages and chops, mix together three cups crushed corn flakes and half a packet of French onion soup.

BEFORE cooking rabbit, soak in water with a teaspoon of bicarbonate of soda. It makes the flesh white as well as tender.

USE scissors to cut up fruit for a fruit cake, its easier and quicker.

DON'T forget to take your pills, place them next to your toothbrush.

INSTEAD of throwing out old magazines take them to your doctor's surgery or the hospital. They will be glad of them.

LEFT over dining room wallpaper makes attractive matching table mats. Paste them on cardboard and spray over with plastic spray.

AS a centre piece for the table, float flowers in water, cut stems very short to stabilize.

IF you have an old chiming clock keeps it in good working order, place a container full of kerosene under the works, the fumes lubricates the mechanism.

WHEN serving curry place a plate of cucumber on the table this will soon soothe the palate.

ADD a sprig of mint to your flower arrangements, it will give off a delightful fragrance.

TO colour white flowers, simply place in water with a few drops of food coloring. Leave overnight then remove.

REDUCE bacon shrinkage by coating the slices with flour before frying.

A scallop shell makes an excellent utensil for de-scaling fish, Work from the tail towards the head.

WHEN greasing cake tins and dishes use vegetable oil or lard. This does not contain butter and therefore is less likely to stick.

YOU can get more volume when whisking egg whites if you rub a cut lemon around the inside of the bowl before use.

IF you don't like using hair spray from the can, spray it onto your hairbrush and comb through your hair. This will hold your hair without that sticky look.

USE the colored tops from old ball-point pens as markers for seed rows when planting. Different colours for different seeds and the weather changes don't harm them.

PREVENT birds from eating lettuce and other plants by tying strips of plastic to a length of string above each row, bread bags are good.

TO reheat pancakes without cooking them further, simply wrap them in a clean tea towel and place them in a warm oven for a few minutes; do not leave the oven on or the tea towel could catch alight.

PLACE a stick of celery in the bread bag and it will help to keep it fresh.

LETTUCE will stay fresher longer if you cover the base of the crisper with absorbent paper.
DIP the knife into boiling water before slicing iced

cakes. This will prevent the icing from breaking up.

TO make creases in skirts and trousers sharper, spray the inside of the crease with starch before ironing.

REMOVE old polish buildup from furniture, Sponge with a cloth, wring out in one part vinegar to six parts water.

YOU can remove the rust on metal furniture by rubbing with turpentine. To restore the shine use a car chrome polish.

WHEN ironing velvet always iron on the inside. If you cover the ironing board with a thick towel, it helps protect the velvet from crushing.

BRISTLE brooms will last longer if you dip them in cold salted water before use. And they will keep their shape longer if they are hung up and not left to stand.

TO store scarves and keep them free from wrinkles, wrap them around the cardboard rolls that come with plastic wrap or foil.

USE a vacuum cleaner nozzle to clean out the bobbin area of your sewing machine, cotton dust soon clogs and this will save the maintenance cost.

BEFORE pinning nylon materials, stick the pins into a cake of soap. the pins will then stay in the fabric and not slip out.

ALWAYS remember there are certain household items that are potential killers, especially to small children. So always keep them out of their reach. These include, insecticide, weed killer, household bleach, kerosene, Ammonia, toilet cleaners and drain cleaners to name but a few.

DON'T store poisonous liquids in food containers, especially soft-drink bottles. they are easily mistaken for drink and can be fatal.

BEFORE trying to remove a splinter from a small child's finger, rub it over with an ice cube. The ice helps numb the area slightly and the child will feel less pain.

ALWAYS keep front-loading washing machines closed when not in use to prevent any small children from climbing in and closing the door.

USE fine nylon Venetian blind cord for sand shoe laces for children's shoes. it will outlast twelve pairs of ordinary ones.

USE a biscuit cutter in fancy shapes for cutting party sandwiches for children.

SLIP an old tea cozy over the back of a baby's high chair. This saves many a bump.

A siphon of soda makes an excellent fire extinguisher if the real thing is not around.

SOAK candles in salty water for a few hours before lighting and they won t drip. Allow them to drip dry.

SMEAR a little camphorated oil on the bottom of electric light globes to keep the flies away.

IF you are bothered by flies in the kitchen each time you boil cabbage, simply cook some celery in the same saucepan. Tried and true.

WHEN storing white garments, don't put them in plastic bags, it tends to make them go yellow. Cover them instead with calico.

REMOVE tangles from a child's hair without the pain. Fill a spray bottle with water and add some conditioner, spray while brushing, and the kids will love it.

ELIMINATE noise from scraping chairs on polished or tiled floors; glue some bunion pads to the bottom of the legs. It also prevents the floors from becoming scratched.

BEFORE you paint new wooden items, give them a coat of linseed oil and allow to dry thoroughly, then lightly sandpaper. When you paint over this the finish will be brilliant.

MEND children's toys (if Super Glue is not at hand) by heating up an old knife and run it along the crack, pressing together as you do so.

A medicine glass is excellent for measuring small amounts of food ingredients in your recipes.

WHEN cooking always keep the handles pointing inwards to avoid them from being tipped over.

NEVER use a cutting board on the kitchen sink; if it slips it could cause a nasty injury.

CLEAN the inside of aluminum teapots, place two Sterodent tooth cleaning tablets inside the pot and fill with boiling water. Allow to stand overnight then rub gently with a scourer, it will shine as new.

EXTRACT juice from an onion without the tears, place the onion over a normal lemon squeezer, and squeeze hard.

ADD a slice of lemon when soaking lettuce, this will help crisp the lettuce leaves more quickly.

WHEN cooking apricots add a pinch of

bicarbonate of soda. This kills the acid in the fruit and you will need less sugar.

PLACE a lump of sugar in the cheese dish, it will

help prevent mould and will keep the cheese soft.

IF you smoke tobacco, place a cabbage leaf in the bottom of the tobacco box. It will never dry out.

TO clean glass in your wood stove, use oven cleaner when the glass is cool, it cleans without scratching.

EGG shells placed around your carnations will give them much needed lime.

BLUE tack is great for holding climbing plants to the wall and will not leave any marks.

MAKE a non-toxic garden spray by mixing 4 crushed hot peppers, 4 large onions and 2 bulbs of garlic, cover with water and leave for 24 hours. Strain and add enough water to make 4 liters.

FOR a different pastry crust for fruit pies try mixing 1½ cups plain flour with 1 cup quick cooking oats and salt ...to taste. Rub in 125g soft butter or margarine and mix to a firm dough with cold water. It's delicious.

CACTUS spines are painful if they come in contact with you hands, so always use kitchen tongs when potting to hold the plant in position.

PLAIN yoghurt placed on the skin in an emergency will cool the skin and help relieve the pain.

TO make an economical mock almond icing, substitute 90g of ground rice and one teaspoon of almond essence for ground almonds using your usual recipe for almond paste. Glaze the surface of the cake with sieved apricot jam before applying paste. Almond icing should be dry before other icing is applied.

WHEN you clean your light globes, wipe them over with a cloth dipped in your favorite perfume. The heat will spread the perfume fragrance throughout the room.

TO remove stains from toilet bowls rub over with a paste made with borax and lemon juice.

GET more juice from lemons, warm them and roll them on a table before cutting.

WHEN making cushions, break a piece of camphor into small bits and mix into the filling. This will keep the cushions fresh and keep moths away.

IRONING pleated skirts is made easier and less time-consuming if you gather the pleats with a needle and thread. after pressing, leave the thread in place until the skirt is needed.

WHEN cooking mince, add a handful of rice as this will make the mince go further and helps soak up excess fat.

ADD a pinch of salt to flowers in vases as this will keep the flowers fresher longer and they'll be more vigorous.

AN easy hint to remember for cooking vegetables is, always cook those that grow under the ground covered, and those that grow above ground uncovered.

WHEN using raw onions in a salad, always soak them for 10 minutes in cold water. This prevents the onion odours dominating the dish.

DISGUISE a crack in your favorite dish by simmering it for 45 minutes in sweet milk. The dish will look like new again.

WHEN roasting lamb, mix the juice of a lemon, salt and pepper in a saucer and rub over the lamb before cooking, it's delicious.

A squeeze of lemon juice and sugar rubbed into your hands will make them soft and white.

IF you keep your and fish hooks in jars with rice or baby powder, they will not rust.

PLASTIC flower trays make excellent spill trays for your kettle.

USE a fine nylon tea strainer to dust the tops of cakes and sponges with icing sugar.

BANANAS will not turn brown in fruit salads if you pour boiling water over them before peeling. Allow the skins to turn grey then peel them immediately

IF your custard goes lumpy when you boil it, put about ¼ cup of cold water in and beat it with an egg beater. The lumps should disappear.

IF you live in a flat and your pot plants are short of earth, simply empty your tea leaves and tea bags into them. This will help the plants to thrive.

IF you don't believe in using salt in cooking etc.; add a slice of lemon when boiling vegetables, this will give them a delightful tang.

PADDED postage bags are great for packing your nail polish bottles and cosmetics in when traveling. It will save a lot of messy breakages.

DOUBLE D Eucalyptus oil will remove all stains from clothing and most furniture if applied with a clean cloth.

REMOVE lipstick stains from white handkerchiefs by soaking in vinegar. For colored hankies use equal amounts of vinegar and water.

ALWAYS use a piece of muslin over the top of a mould when a jelly is standing. Anything containing gelatin is particularly dust absorbing.

ADD a drop of glycerin to gum or glue it will prevent it from becoming brittle.

COVER your custard or white sauce with foil; it will prevent skin from forming.

BEFORE painting around windows frames, coat the glass with neat washing-up liquid and allow to dry for a day. Paint spatters will not stick to the glass and can be easily wiped off.

DON'T suffer from smarting teary eyes when peeling onions. Chew on a piece of dry bread when peeling. Sound silly! try it works.

REMOVE mulberry stains from the skin, rub the stains with a green mulberry and watch the stains disappear. And for mulberry stains on clothes, crush a green mulberry, cover the stain with the juice and leave a few minutes before rinsing in cold water.

IF you add too much garlic to a casserole or stew, simply add a sprig of parsley and cook for a few minutes. This will tone down the garlic taste.

CANDLES are always handy to have around. Sticking windows, curtain tracks, drawers, drip hot wax into the slots of a new miter-box and the saw will never stick.

KEEP fully-open roses from falling; spray the backs of the petals with hair spray to hold for a few more days.

SHREDDED cellophane makes an economical and pretty Christmas tree decoration, clear resembles icicles; red and gold add rich colour.

AFTER washing silk, apply fabric spray while still damp and it will iron beautifully.

EMPTY roll-on deodorant bottles are handy for applying sun blocks down on the beach.

TRAYS from biscuit packs are handy for holding party sausages and meatballs in the fridge.

USE little-used perfumes in the bathroom; add a splash to your bath for a fragrant change.

EMPTY tissue boxes make great pencil and crayon cases for children to use during long car journeys.

SAVE your fingers as you hammer home a nail, hold it in place with a dab of your child's plasticine.

POUR medicine away from label side of bottle; it prevents drips from obscuring the dosage instructions.

SAVE trying to locate the end of the sticky tape by placing a small button under the end.

CLEAN white shoes with a little nail polish remover before applying shoe polish for a brand-new finish.

DRESS zipper stuck, sprinkle some talcum powder on it, run up and down a few times and then brush off surplus.

PLASTIC cotton reels threaded on to a strong cord and securely tied make a splendid toy for a toddler to play with.

RIPE bananas may he mashed and frozen to use at a later date when making a banana cake.

REMOVE stubborn streaks from glass shower doors, screw up an old newspaper and pour on a little methylated spirits, your glass will sparkle.

SAVE time looking for lost hair bands, twist them onto the handle of the hair brush.

GRIND some lemon peel into your garbage disposal unit and get rid of all other had odours.

PAINT an old roller blind with blackboard paint to make a very good and cheap chalk board that rolls up out of the way.

THE soft scent from a lavender sachet enclosed in a pillow seems to induce sleep, try it if you have trouble getting to sleep.

PLASTIC cling film will tear easily if stored in the refrigerator.

USE washable fabric paint to give your kids old faded canvas shoe's a new start.

PREVENT your child from running into your glass patio door by sticking colored tape or even motifs across it at their eye level.

IF stitches on dark fabric are hard to see when unpicking, mark them by running up the seam with white chalk.

USE damp string to tie up a parcel securely; as it dries it shrinks and tightens around the parcel.

USE discarded Styrofoam packing, cut to size to make handy notice boards.

PREVENT accidents by sticking sharp ends of skewers into corks before storing away.

SEW two sides of a face washer to make a container for a frozen drink; sandwiches in the lunch box won't be spoilt by condensation.

BEND a strong metal coat hanger so it makes a loop with the hook downwards; place loop over a branch of tree, great for hanging plants from.

CUT the top off of a plastic bottle to fit paint brush handle and you have a good drip catcher, secure with tape.

USE a beer-can opener to make a pouring hole in washing powder boxes.

BRIGHTEN your personnel writing paper by gluing on pressed flowers.

PRESS your biscuit tops with a potato masher for decorative biscuits.

TODDLERS training cups with spouted lids make handy, non-spilling water containers for the sick and elderly people.

SAVE arguments over whose socks and hankies are whose, allocate your family a colour each and put a few small stitches of appropriately colored cotton where it doesn't show.

TIE plastic bags over your slippers when its raining and you want to step outside briefly to pick parsley, mint etc.

A fishing net suspended from the ceiling in a child's room will hold all his toys and he can lie and look up at them whilst falling asleep.

WHEN cooking sausages on your barbecue pin them together with a long skewer. Makes them much easier to turn and keeps them straight.

KEEP an old, long sleeve from a man shirt in the glove box of your car, when driving a long distance use it to protect your arm from sunburn.

KEEP grubs of seedlings by placing cardboard cylinders from toilet rolls etc. over seedlings and pushing into the dirt.

TYPE the names and addresses of family and friends onto sticky labels before going on holidays for quick and easy mailing.

AMUSE your children on a fine day in the garden, fill up a bucket with water and give each a paint

Brush and tell them to paint the house! The bricks will dry in no time.

USE a cut-down drinking straw to steady a large reel or spool of cotton on the sewing machine, also keeps it from falling off.

MAKE an easy hot water bottle cover by sewing some face washers together.

MAKE it easier to thread cotton through a fine needle by applying a small amount of soap to the end of the cotton.

PADDED bags from the post office stuffed with newspaper make great pads to kneel on.

PLACE flour in a large salt shaker to dust your pastry with.

A green pepper that has been hollowed out makes a good novelty holder for dip.

ATTACH a piece of elastic across the inside of a desk drawer to keep the small bottles from falling over each time it's opened.

AFTER cleaning a paint brush, keep it soft by rinsing it in water with added fabric conditioner.

MAKE great book ends by wrapping two bricks in some colorful fabric.

KEEP honey in a squeeze type sauce bottle, easy to dispense with no mess.

ATTACH a couple of coat hooks to the top of a ladder for rags; they will always be in reach.

PATENT leather shoes make them shine with furniture spray-on polish.

USE a golf-tee to pierce a hole in packet salt: makes pouring easy and can be used as a stopper as well.

A child will never forget to hand in a school note if it is taped to his lunch box securely.

USE a pipe cleaner to clean that awkward teapot spout.

FOR very thin cheese slices, use a potato peeler, they will be wafer thin.

AFTER threading a child's shoelaces through the first two holes of the shoe, tie a knot on either side of hole so that laces won t get lost.

TWIST a large rubber band around shampoo container to prevent it from slipping from your grasp while in the shower.

REMOVE scratches from a watch glass face by rubbing gently with some tooth paste.

IN an emergency use a dampened piece of lint free cloth as a substitute clothes brush.

BEAN sprouts last longer if refrigerated in a bowl of water with a few slices of lemon; change water daily.

CREATE a distinctive design with reflective tape on your children's raincoats; it makes the coat easy to identify and the child visible to motorists on dark evenings from school.

A large key-ring attached to a bath plug makes it easy for the elderly and young children to remove the plug after their bath.

KEEP your tea towel at hand by attaching a small piece of Velcro to your apron and the matching piece to the towel.

SAVE the chassis and wheels of an irreparable lawn mower for transporting heavy and bulky objects around the garden.

SAVE a lot of space on the line by hanging nappies and suchlike across two lines instead of along one.

WHEN using the garden sprinkler, set the kitchen cooker alarm clock to remind you to turn it off again.

DON'T chance losing your money or keys at the beach, turn over a corner of your beach towel, sew it up and insert a zip. Keep a sealable plastic bag in the pocket and paper money won't get damp.

WHEN making waist aprons for the elderly or arthritic people, allow for longer ties which can be brought around the waist to the front.

NOTE your appointments on a calendar, then hang it inside your wardrobe; it will remind you as you dress each morning. You will never miss another.

MAKE an extra large zippered cover for your folded Doona and use it as an extra cushion during the summer months. It saves on storage space.

AFTER opening a new tin of paint, use a nail to punch a few holes in the groove around the top of the tin. When the brush is wiped on the lip, excess paint runs back inside the tin not down the outside.

IF children are scared of getting shampoo in their eyes when having their hair washed, let them wear swimming goggles.

STOP laundry powder from getting lumpy and soggy by pouring it into the empty plastic cordial bottles, easy to store and pour. (Remove all labels and remark clearly for safety.)

AN easy way to keep a check on rows of knitting completed is by attaching a paper clip to the pattern and sliding it along as each row is done.

IF a sticky sweet sticks between your teeth, a very hot drink will soon soften it and relieve the discomfort.

KEEP a safety pin on your key ring for that emergency.

WHEN winding a sewing machine bobbin, use colored chalk to mark the first meter of cotton, you'll know when the thread is about to run out.

TREAT table mats with a spray-on fabric protector, for quick and easy cleaning.

CHILDREN learning to knit? Give them different colored needles: white for plain, red for purl, etc., stocking stitch will be conquered with ease.

KEEP your toaster stood inside a plastic tray; it saves a lot of messy crumbs everywhere.

CORNERS cut from old envelopes make simple book markers.

REMOVE smells from jars you wish to keep with by rubbing with on a paste made from water and bicarbonate of soda.

RUN out of laundry powder? grate some laundry soap into the machine while filling with warm water.

DON'T discard old cassette-tape cases; recycle as a business card or photo holder! Simply fold back the clear section of case, glue pivot point to hold and place on a desk with your cards or photo's inside.

SAVE the silica gel packs from vitamin bottles, tape them to the inside of your coffee jar. The coffee will never get damp.

OLD telephone directories are handy for the workshop; tear out pages for wiping up grease, paint or most other things.

DON'T discard the leaves from your celery stalks -dry them, and rub to a powder and put into a jar with a tight fitting lid. This can be used for flavoring soups and stews in the future.

IF you can t get rid of freshly painted paint smells try a saucer full of ammonia in the room overnight. Or a bowl of salt in the room sometimes helps.

RUST on chrome can be removed by crumpling some aluminum foil in your hand, dip it in water and rub the rust off and wipe over with a clean cloth, then apply a good chrome polish.

DURING hot and humid weather, feet become sticky and often cause shoes to retain odours. Simply shake a small amount of bicarbonate of soda into the shoes and ...leave overnight. Shake out well the next day and they will smell fresh again.

SCORCH marks on cotton can be removed by wetting the mark with cold water, make a paste of laundry starch pack over mark until dry. Sponge off with peroxide and place in the sun to dry.

REMOVE stains from a stainless steel sink, mix a tablespoon of cream of tartar with boiling water and pour over stain, wipe thoroughly. Vinegar is also excellent for cleaning stainless steel sinks, simply wipe over whole sink with a cloth moistened in vinegar.

IF you have just had a glass of milk rinse in cold water before washing in warm, it prevents a dull look.

IF you have tar marks on your car try washing over with a cloth dipped in kerosene or white spirits, then wash and polish in the usual way.

IF you have synthetic bed linen or blankets that hold static electricity, try adding some fabric softener to the rinse water it should help to reduce it.

I hope there were some tips that helped you.

On the following pages you can add
Your own tips.

<u>NOTES</u>

<u>NOTES</u>

<u>NOTES</u>

www.ingramcontent.com/pod-product-compliance
Lightning Source LLC
Chambersburg PA
CBHW060413290526
45791CB00002B/724